Alex Kent & Jen Smith

BIG Guide to Tapping

Positive EFT Emotional Freedom Techniques for Children

This book is dedicated to Amber, Ottilie and the next-generation of children who'll grow up emotionally smart thanks to tapping pioneers Roger Callahan, Gary Craig & Silvia Hartmann.

www.DragonRising.com

Hello!

My name is **BIG** Ted and I will show you how to tap with your magic finger to recharge your battery and feel great.

Show me your magic finger...

That's it!

Sunshine

Fun

Big

Brave

Strong

Amazing

Adventure

Good

Smile

Happy

Friend

Excited

Bouncy

Yummy

Magic

Love

Play

Clever

Beautiful

Sing

Now choose a magic word you want more of...

Say it out loud!

Now let us get ready.

Cross both your hands over your heart and take 3 deep breaths:

In... Out...

In... Out...

In... Out...

Say your magic word!

When you say your magic word, how full is your battery?

Show me with your magic finger.

Now let us do the tapping to put more energy in...

Now with your magic finger...

Tap gently on each of the points...

From top to bottom...

And say your magic word on each one.

Great!

Now to tap your hand...

Again, with your magic finger...

Tap gently on each of the hand points...

From top to bottom...

And say your magic word on each one.

To finish the tapping, cross both your hands over your heart and take 3 deep breaths:

In... Out...

In... Out...

In... Out...

How full is your battery now?

Show me with your magic finger.

Well done!

You have just completed your magic tapping.

Tap again to put even more energy in your battery.

Magic Tapping 1-2-3:

1. Cross both hands over your heart, take three deep breaths and say your magic word

2. Tap your magic points from top to bottom with your magic finger. On each one say your magic word

3. Cross both hands over your heart and take three deep breaths

Well-done!

Remember to do your magic tapping every time your battery needs a top-up.

Keep tapping and see you soon!

Information For Grownups

Since its development at the turn of the last century, Classic Emotional Freedom Techniques (EFT) has helped many tens of thousands of people, both young and old, release unwanted emotions from their day-to-day lives.

In 2013, Silvia Hartmann who is a UK researcher and current chairperson of The Association for Meridian & Energy Therapies (The AMT) further developed the classic method into Positive EFT which is far more suited to working with children.

Rather than having young people focus or dwell on the negative, we instead ask them what they would like more of and then use Hartmann's "Heart & Soul" Energy EFT tapping protocol to increase energy flow until the negative is replaced by the positive.

Tips:

- Tap along with the child so they can follow your lead. Remember to encourage/praise at every stage

- The positive words in balloons are just examples. It is more effective to use the child's own words

- If you're using EFT for a problem then encourage the child to pick the positive antidote. For example, use "Happy" instead of "Sad", "Brave" instead of "Scared", etc.

- Very young children may not understand the battery concept for gauging their progress. Feel free to skip this stage if necessary

- When tapping the finger points aim for the side of the finger nail

- Yawning is a sign that your child's "battery" is about half-full so try not to stop at this stage, unless you want them to go to sleep!

- Make it fun. Tapping should be a joy!

Further Information...

The Association for Meridian & Energy Therapies (The AMT) is a not-for-profit organisation which holds a world-wide register of fully trained, certified and insured Positive EFT Practitioners and EFT Master Practitioners.

If you'd like to contact a practitioner for an EFT session (either in person, by telephone or skype), or would like professional EFT training for yourself or a group then please visit the website: **www.TheAMT.com**

Recommended Reading...

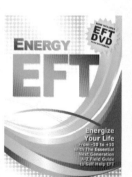

Positive EFT by Silvia Hartmann

In this easy-to-read book you'll discover Silvia Hartmann's Positive EFT and experience many ideas for increasing the energy flow on what you want, thus leading to happier and more fulfilled lives.

Energy EFT by Silvia Hartmann

Energy EFT is the comprehensive guide to modern EFT and is written in a friendly, practical yet content rich format. Suitable for beginners right through to EFT Master Practitioners, you'll want to dip in & out time and time again to learn something new.

Energy EFT comes complete with 90 minutes of video making it fabulous value.

Find these books and more by Silvia Hartmann:
www.DragonRising.com

Thank-You!

Remember to tell your friends and family about BIG Ted whenever they look like they need cheering up. He will help turn sad into happy and happy into super-happy.

Happy Tapping!

For free BIG Ted resources, training materials and customer support please contact DragonRising Publishing:

staff@DragonRising.com

www.DragonRising.com

Made in the USA
Lexington, KY
18 July 2014